The Best I Can Be
Living With Fetal Alcohol Syndrome/Effects

by Liz Kulp

co-written by Jodee Kulp

(Revised 2009)

Dedicated to:

Prenatally alcohol exposed children of the world.

At first I was mad.
Now I know I am not responsible
for getting fetal alcohol syndrome,
but I have to learn to live with it.

I think life is hard . . .
but I can't quit.

Table of Contents

Thank You

Liz and I would like to thank our Heavenly Father and all the professionals and families who are loving, working and doing research for children and persons with Fetal Alcohol Syndrome and Effects for making this book possible. We would especially like to thank the following persons for investing their time and efforts into helping Liz grow: Cathy Bruer-Thompson, Nancy Liebeg, Norman and Bev Benson, Dr. Carrie Kulp, Lauren and David Runnion-Bareford, Kathy Kienzle, Jay and Jeanne Patterson, Jeff and Kathy Haley, Greg and Dianne Olson, Robin and Jim Hokanson, Liv Horneland, JoAnn Kraft, Dr. Jeff Brist, Dr. Elizabeth Reeve, Toni Hager, Dr. Don Sealock and Dr. John Nash.

We thank all the people on Faslink who have contributed quotes within the pages of this book and special thanks to Karl Kulp, Barbara Moores, Corinne Barnwell, Joyce Russell and Donna Getts.

To Better Lives . . . Liz and Jodee Kulp – April 2000

September 2005 – We have added an epilogue on Liz's growth and beginning adulthood.

February 2009 – We have revised Liz's epilogue – She is living interdependently. She is 22.

Preface

It was a beautiful fall morning, the colors of the day shone into our homeschool classroom when Liz asked, *"Mom, do you make money on your* Families at Risk *book?"*

"Some", I answered, *"but more importantly the book has given hope to hundreds of families who need help loving and understanding special adopted kids like you."*

"Mom, I want to write a book about what it's like to have FASD (Fetal Alcohol Spectrum Disorders) *I think people need to know, and I need money."*

Oh, Lord help me, this child is serious. I don't even know how to begin a book like this with her as the author. I prayed silently. We're going to need help, big help! A sense of quiet came over our day as I replied, *"You know what Liz? That's a great idea. I think so too. Let's find out everything we can and you can write your book. The helpers will come for us."*

And so we sat with recipe cards and pencils and I began writing as Liz talked about what it feels like to live with FASD. The days passed and the cards stacked up. We began to sort our notes into little piles and discovered they began to tell a story – not just Liz's story, but the story of many individuals living with brains injured before they were even born.

We continued to talk and write, until finally our little stack seemed complete. And then laboriously Liz began writing, exhausted after only two cards – her story. The story of thousands of other children and adults. And she was right. It is a story worth sharing. And we did need to tell the whole world.

"In 1999, it took Liz 30 minutes to copy two pages of this book. In 2004, she rapped and wrote poetry. In 2009 she lives interdependently."

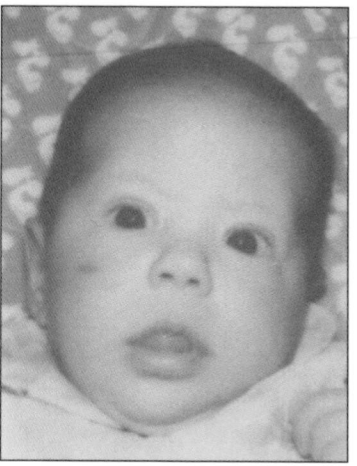

Liz at four months prior to
joining our family.

Liz's High School Graduation
Class of 2004.

WiNN aor finds Do someing
you Sobe not Do Dot go
aloge wich it Like going in ohe
moms Room with finns tath is
not good to Do, and Do
not Koss the srit win our finds
dos, Becuse the may Be coming
Look for cans. And Wins 2 polke

Liz's handwriting at the end of 4th grade.

2009 NOTE:

*Liz now 22, is living
on her own with
supported services to
help her in her early
adult interdependence.*

Liz (3), Mom and
David (15 mos.)

Dave (15) and
Liz (17)

Liz's Adoption Day - 14
months with Mom and Dad.

Our family life is filled with adventures and experiences that we hope can contribute to your family's success and happiness.

Welcome *to our family.
We have chosen to share
our life experiences of Fetal
Alcohol Spectrum Disorder
(FASD) in hopes that other
children and their families
can grow, learn to love life
and not quit. Alcohol use is
one of the primary reasons
that parents can no longer
care for their children and
some of these children are
then placed in foster care
or special needs adoption.
It is estimated that 78%
of children in U.S. foster
care suffer from prenatal
alcohol exposure. At least
40,000 US babies will be
born with FASD* (May, P.A.,
Gossage, J.P. 2001) *and cost
the USA up to $6 billion.*
(Lupton, C; Burd, L and Harwood
R. 2004) *1 in 10 pregnant
women drinks alcohol.*
(CDC, 2004).

*For those special
children with FASD and
their families, Liz and I
hope to make a difference.*

Kulp family

www.betterendings.or